Easy Charcuterie Boards

Simple and Elegant Recipes for Every Occasion

By

Grace U. Langley

Book Contents

CHAPTER 8: SWEET BREADS

CHAPTER 9: SAUCES, CONDIMENTS & DIPS FOR CHARCUTERIE BOARDS

CONCLUSION

Introduction

Welcome to the world of charcuterie boards, where craftsmanship meets appetite in the most wonderful way possible. Whether you're hosting a gathering, having a nice night in, or simply desiring a sophisticated snack, charcuterie boards offer a varied and visually attractive culinary experience.

In this booklet, "Easy Charcuterie Boards," we explore the skill of creating elegantly curated boards that easily merge flavors, textures, and colors. From the beginnings of charcuterie and its progression into the popular board format, to practical recommendations on selecting the finest ingredients and arranging them with grace, this book is your guide to mastering the art of charcuterie.

Discover a variety of board types, from conventional assortments of cured meats and cheeses to unique combinations that cater to varied tastes and dietary preferences. Whether you're a seasoned entertainer trying to boost your hosting game or a rookie chef eager to amaze with minimal effort, the recipes and ideas given here will inspire and empower you to create magnificent charcuterie boards that are as wonderful to behold as they are to enjoy in.

Join us on a journey through flavors and presentation techniques that will convert your dining experience into a memorable occasion. Let's go into the world of "Easy Charcuterie Boards" and learn the secrets to constructing boards that are as delicious as they are visually attractive.

Let's start creating, sharing, and experiencing these delicious moments together!

Chapter 1

What is Charcuterie Board?

A charcuterie board is a carefully curated presentation of cured meats, cheeses, accompaniments, and sometimes other savory or sweet foods, attractively placed on a serving board or platter. The name "charcuterie" stems from the French word "chair" (flesh) and "cuit" (cooked), historically referring to the preparation of cured meats such as salami, prosciutto, and sausages.

History and Origins

The technique of charcuterie dates back centuries, starting in Europe as a means of preserving meats before refrigeration. Early practitioners devised procedures such as curing, smoking, and fermenting to extend the shelf life of meats, which eventually grew into a culinary art form known for its rich flavors and textures.

In France, charcuterie became synonymous with the trade of producing preserved meats, with each area boasting its own specialties and techniques. Italian cuisine also embraces charcuterie with classic cured meats like prosciutto and mortadella, showing a varied spectrum of flavors and styles.

Over time, charcuterie boards have evolved beyond conventional preservation methods into a symbol of conviviality and culinary artistry. Today, these boards are not just a delectable array of flavors but also a visual feast, often decked with fresh fruits, nuts, artisanal cheeses, pickles, olives, and spreads, boosting both taste and beauty.

Why Charcuterie Boards?

Charcuterie boards have soared in popularity due to their variety, simplicity, and ability to accommodate to a wide range of tastes and dietary preferences. Here are a few reasons why charcuterie boards have become a favored choice for gatherings and informal dining:

- Versatility: Charcuterie boards may be adjusted to satisfy diverse dietary needs and tastes, making them perfect for practically any occasion—from private gatherings to big celebrations.
- Ease of Preparation: They need less cooking and preparation time, allowing hosts to focus on presentation and mingling rather than spending hours in the kitchen.

- Visual Appeal: Charcuterie boards are visually attractive, frequently boasting an array of colors, textures, and forms that make them a centerpiece of any table or gathering.
- Flavor Exploration: They offer an opportunity to explore a variety of flavors—from savory cured meats to tangy cheeses and sweet or spicy accompaniments—all in one wonderful spread.
- Social Sharing: Charcuterie boards encourage sharing and sampling, promoting a community dining experience where guests can interact and discover new sensations together.

Essential Tools and Ingredients

Creating a gorgeous charcuterie board takes the correct tools and a selection of high-quality ingredients. Here's everything you'll need to get started:

Tools Needed:

- Serving Board or plate: Choose a board or plate large enough to organize all your ingredients without overcrowding.
- little Bowls or Ramekins: These are handy for containing spreads, dips, or little foods like olives and nuts.
- Cheese Knives and Spreaders: Essential for cutting and serving cheeses and spreads.
- Sharp Knife: For slicing meats and bigger cheeses.
- Decorative Picks or Skewers: Useful for picking up little items like fruits or cheese cubes.
- Garnishing Tools: Optional but handy for adding ornamental touches like fresh herbs or edible flowers.

Selecting Meats:

- Cured Meats: Choose a choice of cured meats such as prosciutto, salami, chorizo, or coppa. Aim for a combination of flavors and textures, from mild to robust.
- Choosing Cheeses:
- Cheese Variety: Select a broad assortment of cheeses, including soft, semi-soft, and hard cheeses. Examples include brie, gouda, cheddar, blue cheese, and goat cheese. Consider several milk types (cow, goat, sheep) for diversity.

Accompaniments (Fruits, Nuts, etc.):

- Fresh Fruits: Include seasonal fruits like grapes, figs, berries, or slices of apple and pear.
- Nuts: Choose a selection of nuts such as almonds, walnuts, or pistachios for crunch and texture.
- Dips and Spreads: Include a variety of spreads like honey, mustard, fig jam, or olive tapenade for extra flavor pairings.
- Pickles and Olives: These give a tart and briny contrast to the richness of meats and cheeses.

This section includes critical information on why charcuterie boards are popular and discusses the tools and ingredients needed to build them, setting the stage for readers to begin planning and assembling their own tasty boards.

Chapter 2: Basic Charcuterie Board Recipes

Classic Cheese and Meat Board

- **Prep Time:** 15 minutes
- **Serving Size:** 4-6 people

Ingredients:

- Assorted cured meats (such as prosciutto, salami, and coppa)
- Variety of cheeses (e.g., brie, cheddar, blue cheese)
- Grapes or figs
- Nuts (almonds, walnuts)
- Crackers or breadsticks
- Mustard and honey for dipping

Instructions:

1. Arrange the cured meats and cheeses on a large serving board or platter.
2. Place clusters of grapes or figs around the board.
3. Scatter nuts between the meats and cheeses.
4. Add crackers or breadsticks to fill in empty spaces.
5. Serve with small bowls of mustard and honey for dipping.

Mediterranean Inspired Board

- **Prep Time:** 20 minutes
- **Serving Size:** 4-6 people

Ingredients:

- Sliced chorizo and prosciutto
- Manchego and feta cheese
- Olives (kalamata and green)

- Cherry tomatoes

- Marinated artichoke hearts

- Bread or crostini

Instructions:

1. Arrange the sliced meats and cheeses on a board.

2. Place olives and cherry tomatoes in small piles around the board.

3. Arrange marinated artichoke hearts in a corner of the board.

4. Serve with slices of bread or crostini.

Vegetarian Board

- **Prep Time:** 15 minutes

- **Serving Size:** 4-6 people

Ingredients:

- Assorted cheeses (such as brie, goat cheese, and gouda)

- Hummus

- Fresh vegetables (carrots, cucumbers, cherry tomatoes)

- Mixed nuts (almonds, cashews)

- Grapes

- Crackers

Instructions:

1. Arrange the assorted cheeses on a board.

2. Place small bowls of hummus and mixed nuts on the board.

3. Arrange fresh vegetables around the cheeses.

4. Scatter grapes on the board.

5. Serve with crackers.

Smoked Salmon Board
- **Prep Time:** 15 minutes
- **Serving Size:** 4-6 people

Ingredients:

- Smoked salmon slices
- Cream cheese
- Capers
- Red onion, thinly sliced
- Lemon wedges
- Bagels or bread

Instructions:

1. Arrange smoked salmon slices on a board.
2. Place small bowls of cream cheese and capers on the board.
3. Scatter thinly sliced red onion around the salmon.
4. Serve with lemon wedges and toasted bagels or bread.

French Inspired Board
- **Prep Time:** 20 minutes
- **Serving Size:** 4-6 people

Ingredients:

- Jambon (French ham)
- Brie and camembert cheese
- Cornichons (small pickles)
- Dijon mustard
- Baguette slices

Instructions:

1. Arrange slices of jambon on a board.

2. Place wedges of brie and camembert cheese on the board.

3. Scatter cornichons around the meats and cheeses.

4. Serve with small bowls of Dijon mustard and slices of baguette.

Italian Antipasto Board

- **Prep Time:** 15 minutes

- **Serving Size:** 4-6 people

Ingredients:

- Prosciutto and salami slices

- Mozzarella balls

- Cherry tomatoes

- Basil leaves

- Balsamic glaze

- Breadsticks or Italian bread

Instructions:

1. Arrange prosciutto and salami slices on a board.

2. Place mozzarella balls and cherry tomatoes around the board.

3. Garnish with fresh basil leaves.

4. Drizzle with balsamic glaze.

5. Serve with breadsticks or slices of Italian bread.

Nutty Cheese Board

- **Prep Time:** 15 minutes
- **Serving Size:** 4-6 people

Ingredients:

- Gouda and cheddar cheese
- Mixed nuts (pecans, almonds)
- Dried apricots
- Honey
- Crackers or crusty bread

Instructions:

1. Arrange slices of gouda and cheddar cheese on a board.
2. Scatter mixed nuts and dried apricots around the cheeses.
3. Drizzle honey over the cheeses.
4. Serve with crackers or crusty bread.

Sweet & Savory Board

- **Prep Time:** 20 minutes
- **Serving Size:** 4-6 people

Ingredients:

- Sliced prosciutto and turkey
- Brie and blue cheese
- Fresh figs
- Honeycomb or honey
- Dark chocolate squares
- Baguette slices

Instructions:

1. Arrange slices of prosciutto and turkey on a board.

2. Place wedges of brie and blue cheese on the board.

3. Scatter fresh figs and dark chocolate squares around the board.

4. Serve with honeycomb or drizzle honey over the cheeses.

5. Serve with baguette slices.

Spicy Charcuterie Board

- **Prep Time:** 15 minutes

- **Serving Size:** 4-6 people

Ingredients:

- Spicy salami and pepperoni slices

- Pepper jack and aged cheddar cheese

- Jalapeño peppers (fresh or pickled)

- Spicy nuts (such as spiced almonds)

- Crackers or flatbread

Instructions:

1. Arrange spicy salami and pepperoni slices on a board.

2. Place slices of pepper jack and aged cheddar cheese on the board.

3. Scatter jalapeño peppers and spicy nuts around the board.

4. Serve with crackers or flatbread.

---

10. Breakfast Charcuterie Board

- **Prep Time:** 20 minutes

- **Serving Size:** 4-6 people

Ingredients:

- Sliced ham and turkey bacon
- Scrambled eggs
- Mini pancakes or waffles
- Fresh berries (strawberries, blueberries)
- Maple syrup
- Toast or English muffins

Instructions:

1. Arrange slices of ham and turkey bacon on a board.
2. Place small piles of scrambled eggs and mini pancakes or waffles on the board.
3. Scatter fresh berries around the board.
4. Serve with maple syrup and toast or English muffins.

Chapter 3: Advanced Charcuterie Board Recipes

International Flavors Board

- **Prep Time:** 25 minutes
- **Serving Size:** 4-6 people

Ingredients:

- Sliced serrano ham (Spanish)
- Manchego and aged cheddar cheese
- Marcona almonds (Spanish)
- Quince paste
- Breadsticks or crusty bread

Instructions:

1. Arrange serrano ham slices on a board.
2. Place wedges of Manchego and aged cheddar cheese on the board.
3. Scatter Marcona almonds around the meats and cheeses.
4. Serve with quince paste and breadsticks or crusty bread.

Seafood Delight Board

- **Prep Time:** 30 minutes
- **Serving Size:** 4-6 people

Ingredients:

- Smoked salmon and trout slices
- Cream cheese with dill
- Capers and pickled onions
- Lemon wedges
- Pumpernickel bread or bagels

Instructions:

1. Arrange smoked salmon and trout slices on a board.

2. Place a bowl of cream cheese with dill in the center of the board.

3. Scatter capers and pickled onions around the seafood.

4. Serve with lemon wedges and pumpernickel bread or bagels.

Dessert Charcuterie Board

- **Prep Time:** 20 minutes
- **Serving Size:** 4-6 people

Ingredients:

- Sliced prosciutto and figs
- Brie and mascarpone cheese
- Honey and raspberry preserves
- Fresh berries (strawberries, raspberries)
- Chocolate truffles

Instructions:

1. Arrange slices of prosciutto and figs on a board.

2. Place wedges of brie and dollops of mascarpone cheese on the board.

3. Drizzle honey and raspberry preserves over the cheeses and figs.

4. Scatter fresh berries and chocolate truffles around the board.

Asian Fusion Board

- **Prep Time:** 25 minutes
- **Serving Size:** 4-6 people

Ingredients:

- Sliced duck breast and teriyaki beef
- Wasabi peas and pickled ginger
- Edamame beans
- Sushi rice crackers
- Soy sauce and spicy mayo

Instructions:

1. Arrange slices of duck breast and teriyaki beef on a board.
2. Place bowls of wasabi peas and pickled ginger on the board.
3. Scatter edamame beans and sushi rice crackers around the meats.
4. Serve with small bowls of soy sauce and spicy mayo.

Artisanal Cheese Board

- **Prep Time:** 20 minutes
- **Serving Size:** 4-6 people

Ingredients:

- Aged gouda and stilton cheese
- Fig and walnut bread
- Dried apricots and cherries
- Honeycomb
- Candied pecans

Instructions:

1. Arrange slices of aged gouda and stilton cheese on a board.

2. Place slices of fig and walnut bread around the cheeses.

3. Scatter dried apricots, cherries, and candied pecans around the board.

4. Serve with chunks of honeycomb.

Vegan Delight Board

- **Prep Time:** 20 minutes
- **Serving Size:** 4-6 people

Ingredients:

- Vegan charcuterie (such as seitan or tempeh)
- Vegan cheeses (cashew cheese, almond cheese)
- Fresh vegetables (bell peppers, cherry tomatoes)
- Hummus and olive tapenade
- Gluten-free crackers

Instructions:

1. Arrange slices of vegan charcuterie and cheeses on a board.

2. Place fresh vegetables and small bowls of hummus and olive tapenade on the board.

3. Serve with gluten-free crackers.

Exotic Fruit and Cheese Board

- **Prep Time:** 25 minutes
- **Serving Size:** 4-6 people

Ingredients:

- Dragon fruit and starfruit slices
- Halloumi and goat cheese
- Mango chutney and passionfruit jam
- Macadamia nuts
- Coconut crackers

Instructions:

1. Arrange slices of dragon fruit and starfruit on a board.
2. Place slices of halloumi and goat cheese on the board.
3. Drizzle mango chutney and passionfruit jam over the cheeses and fruits.
4. Scatter macadamia nuts around the board.
5. Serve with coconut crackers.

Rustic Italian Board

- **Prep Time:** 30 minutes
- **Serving Size:** 4-6 people

Ingredients:

- Prosciutto and pancetta slices
- Pecorino and taleggio cheese
- Sun-dried tomatoes and marinated artichokes
- Breadsticks and focaccia
- Balsamic glaze

Instructions:

1. Arrange prosciutto and pancetta slices on a board.

2. Place wedges of pecorino and taleggio cheese on the board.

3. Scatter sun-dried tomatoes and marinated artichokes around the meats and cheeses.

4. Serve with breadsticks, focaccia, and a drizzle of balsamic glaze.

Southwestern Fiesta Board

- **Prep Time:** 25 minutes

- **Serving Size:** 4-6 people

Ingredients:

- Chorizo and carne asada slices

- Pepper jack and cotija cheese

- Roasted corn and black bean salsa

- Jalapeño slices and lime wedges

- Tortilla chips

Instructions:

1. Arrange chorizo and carne asada slices on a board.

2. Place slices of pepper jack and crumbled cotija cheese on the board.

3. Scatter roasted corn and black bean salsa around the meats and cheeses.

4. Garnish with jalapeño slices and lime wedges.

5. Serve with tortilla chips.

Elegant French Board

- **Prep Time:** 30 minutes
- **Serving Size:** 4-6 people

Ingredients:

- Foie gras and duck rillettes
- Camembert and bleu d'Auvergne cheese
- Fig compote and truffle honey
- Toasted baguette slices
- Champagne grapes

Instructions:

1. Arrange slices of foie gras and spoonfuls of duck rillettes on a board.
2. Place wedges of camembert and crumbled bleu d'Auvergne cheese on the board.
3. Drizzle fig compote and truffle honey over the cheeses and spreads.
4. Serve with toasted baguette slices and Champagne grapes.

Chapter 4: Special Occasion Boards

Holiday Celebration Board

- **Prep Time:** 30 minutes

- **Serving Size:** 6-8 people

Ingredients:

- Sliced honey ham and turkey breast

- Brie and cranberry goat cheese

- Cranberry sauce and honey mustard

- Fresh cranberries and pomegranate seeds

- Assorted crackers and bread

Instructions:

1. Arrange slices of honey ham and turkey breast on a large board or platter.

2. Place wedges of brie and dollops of cranberry goat cheese around the meats.

3. Serve with bowls of cranberry sauce and honey mustard for dipping.

4. Scatter fresh cranberries and pomegranate seeds over the board.

5. Serve with assorted crackers and bread.

Wedding Elegance Board

- **Prep Time:** 40 minutes

- **Serving Size:** 10-12 people

Ingredients:

- Prosciutto and smoked salmon slices

- Brie and aged gouda cheese

- Fig jam and truffle honey

- Fresh figs and grapes

- Crusty baguette and gourmet crackers

Instructions:

1. Arrange slices of prosciutto and smoked salmon in an elegant pattern on a large board.

2. Place wedges of brie and aged gouda cheese around the meats.

3. Drizzle fig jam and truffle honey over the cheeses and meats.

4. Scatter fresh figs and grapes around the board.

5. Serve with slices of crusty baguette and gourmet crackers.

Summer Garden Party Board

- **Prep Time:** 25 minutes
- **Serving Size:** 6-8 people

Ingredients:

- Sliced grilled chicken and prosciutto
- Fresh mozzarella and herb-marinated feta cheese
- Pesto and sun-dried tomato spread
- Cherry tomatoes and cucumber slices
- Ciabatta bread and breadsticks

Instructions:

1. Arrange slices of grilled chicken and prosciutto on a board.

2. Place balls of fresh mozzarella and chunks of herb-marinated feta cheese around the meats.

3. Serve with bowls of pesto and sun-dried tomato spread for dipping.

4. Scatter cherry tomatoes and cucumber slices over the board.

5. Serve with slices of ciabatta bread and breadsticks.

Birthday Bash Board

- **Prep Time:** 30 minutes
- **Serving Size:** 8-10 people

Ingredients:

- Pepperoni and spicy capicola slices
- Sharp cheddar and pepper jack cheese
- Spicy mustard and honey
- Assorted pickles and olives
- Pretzel rods and garlic bread slices

Instructions:

1. Arrange slices of pepperoni and spicy capicola on a board.
2. Place chunks of sharp cheddar and slices of pepper jack cheese around the meats.
3. Serve with bowls of spicy mustard and honey for dipping.
4. Scatter assorted pickles and olives over the board.
5. Serve with pretzel rods and slices of garlic bread.

New Year's Eve Extravaganza Board

- **Prep Time:** 35 minutes
- **Serving Size:** 10-12 people

Ingredients:

- Smoked duck and venison sausage slices
- Blue cheese and aged cheddar cheese
- Fig preserves and wildflower honey
- Mixed nuts and dried fruits

- Sliced baguette and gourmet crackers

Instructions:

1. Arrange slices of smoked duck and venison sausage on a large board.

2. Place wedges of blue cheese and aged cheddar cheese around the meats.

3. Drizzle fig preserves and wildflower honey over the cheeses and meats.

4. Scatter mixed nuts and dried fruits over the board.

5. Serve with sliced baguette and gourmet crackers.

Easter Brunch Board

- **Prep Time:** 30 minutes
- **Serving Size:** 6-8 people

Ingredients:

- Sliced ham and turkey breast
- Swiss and provolone cheese
- Dijon mustard and raspberry jam
- Hard-boiled eggs and pickled asparagus
- Croissants and mini muffins

Instructions:

1. Arrange slices of ham and turkey breast on a board.

2. Place slices of Swiss and provolone cheese around the meats.

3. Serve with bowls of Dijon mustard and raspberry jam for spreading.

4. Scatter halved hard-boiled eggs and pickled asparagus over the board.

5. Serve with croissants and mini muffins.

Fall Harvest Feast Board

- **Prep Time:** 25 minutes
- **Serving Size:** 6-8 people

Ingredients:

- Roast beef and pancetta slices
- Aged gouda and asiago cheese
- Apple butter and maple syrup
- Sliced apples and pears
- Multigrain bread and cinnamon crackers

Instructions:

1. Arrange slices of roast beef and pancetta on a board.
2. Place wedges of aged gouda and asiago cheese around the meats.
3. Drizzle apple butter and maple syrup over the cheeses and meats.
4. Scatter sliced apples and pears over the board.
5. Serve with multigrain bread and cinnamon crackers.

Thanksgiving Bounty Board

- **Prep Time:** 40 minutes
- **Serving Size:** 10-12 people

Ingredients:

- Roasted turkey and cranberry turkey sausage slices
- Brie and smoked gouda cheese
- Cranberry sauce and pumpkin butter
- Candied pecans and dried cranberries
- Cornbread and whole wheat rolls

Instructions:

1. Arrange slices of roasted turkey and cranberry turkey sausage on a large board.

2. Place wedges of brie and smoked gouda cheese around the meats.

3. Serve with bowls of cranberry sauce and pumpkin butter for spreading.

4. Scatter candied pecans and dried cranberries over the board.

5. Serve with slices of cornbread and whole wheat rolls.

Christmas Charcuterie Board

- **Prep Time:** 35 minutes
- **Serving Size:** 8-10 people

Ingredients:

- Glazed ham and venison salami slices
- Cheddar and goat cheese
- Fig jam and cranberry chutney
- Fresh grapes and pomegranate arils
- Rosemary crackers and gingerbread cookies

Instructions:

1. Arrange slices of glazed ham and venison salami on a board.

2. Place chunks of cheddar and crumbled goat cheese around the meats.

3. Drizzle fig jam and cranberry chutney over the cheeses and meats.

4. Scatter fresh grapes and pomegranate arils over the board.

5. Serve with rosemary crackers and gingerbread cookies.

Fourth of July Patriotic Board

- **Prep Time:** 30 minutes

- **Serving Size:** 6-8 people

Ingredients:

- BBQ pulled pork and grilled chicken slices

- Monterey jack and American cheese

- BBQ sauce and ranch dressing

- Cherry tomatoes and blueberries

- Pretzel buns and cornbread muffins

Instructions:

1. Arrange slices of BBQ pulled pork and grilled chicken on a board.

2. Place slices of Monterey jack and American cheese around the meats.

3. Serve with bowls of BBQ sauce and ranch dressing for dipping.

4. Scatter cherry tomatoes and blueberries over the board.

5. Serve with pretzel buns and cornbread muffins.

Chapter 5: Vegetarians Charcuterie Board Recipes

Mediterranean Mezze Board

- **Prep Time:** 20 minutes

- **Serving Size:** 4-6 people

Ingredients:

- Hummus

- Tzatziki

- Falafel balls

- Stuffed grape leaves (dolmas)

- Cherry tomatoes

- Kalamata olives

- Cucumber slices

- Pita bread or crackers

Instructions:

1. Arrange bowls of hummus and tzatziki on a large serving board or platter.

2. Place falafel balls and stuffed grape leaves (dolmas) around the bowls.

3. Scatter cherry tomatoes, kalamata olives, and cucumber slices over the board.

4. Serve with pita bread or crackers for dipping.

Cheese Lover's Board

- **Prep Time:** 15 minutes
- **Serving Size:** 4-6 people

Ingredients:

- Brie cheese
- Goat cheese
- Blue cheese
- Fresh mozzarella balls
- Mixed nuts (such as almonds and walnuts)
- Fresh berries (strawberries and raspberries)
- Honey or fig jam
- Sliced baguette or crackers

Instructions:

1. Arrange slices and wedges of brie, goat cheese, and blue cheese on a board.
2. Place fresh mozzarella balls in a small bowl or ramekin.
3. Scatter mixed nuts and fresh berries around the cheeses.
4. Drizzle honey or spread fig jam over the cheeses.
5. Serve with sliced baguette or crackers.

Greek-Inspired Board

- **Prep Time:** 20 minutes
- **Serving Size:** 4-6 people

Ingredients:

- Feta cheese
- Halloumi cheese (grilled or pan-fried)
- Marinated olives (green and kalamata)
- Roasted red peppers
- Artichoke hearts
- Cherry tomatoes
- Pita bread or breadsticks

Instructions:

1. Arrange blocks of feta cheese and slices of grilled or pan-fried halloumi on a board.
2. Place bowls of marinated olives, roasted red peppers, and artichoke hearts on the board.
3. Scatter cherry tomatoes around the cheeses and bowls.
4. Serve with pita bread or breadsticks.

Caprese Salad Board

- **Prep Time:** 15 minutes
- **Serving Size:** 4-6 people

Ingredients:

- Fresh mozzarella balls
- Cherry tomatoes
- Fresh basil leaves

- Balsamic glaze

- Extra virgin olive oil

- Sea salt and black pepper

- Sliced baguette or ciabatta bread

Instructions:

1. Arrange fresh mozzarella balls, cherry tomatoes, and fresh basil leaves on a board.

2. Drizzle balsamic glaze and extra virgin olive oil over the mozzarella and tomatoes.

3. Sprinkle with sea salt and black pepper to taste.

4. Serve with sliced baguette or ciabatta bread.

Mexican Fiesta Board

- **Prep Time:** 20 minutes

- **Serving Size:** 4-6 people

Ingredients:

- Guacamole

- Salsa

- Refried beans

- Queso fresco or cotija cheese

- Jalapeño slices

- Cherry tomatoes

- Tortilla chips

Instructions:

1. Arrange bowls of guacamole, salsa, and refried beans on a board.

2. Crumble queso fresco or cotija cheese over the bowls.

3. Scatter jalapeño slices and cherry tomatoes around the bowls.

4. Serve with tortilla chips for dipping.

Italian Antipasti Board

- **Prep Time:** 20 minutes

- **Serving Size:** 4-6 people

Ingredients:

- Mozzarella balls (bocconcini)

- Marinated artichoke hearts

- Roasted red peppers

- Sun-dried tomatoes

- Basil pesto

- Grilled or marinated vegetables (zucchini, eggplant)

- Breadsticks or crusty bread

Instructions:

1. Arrange mozzarella balls, marinated artichoke hearts, roasted red peppers, and sun-dried tomatoes on a board.

2. Place a bowl of basil pesto in the center of the board.

3. Scatter grilled or marinated vegetables around the board.

4. Serve with breadsticks or crusty bread.

Asian-Inspired Board

- **Prep Time:** 20 minutes
- **Serving Size:** 4-6 people

Ingredients:

- Edamame beans (steamed and salted)
- Sushi rice
- Avocado slices
- Pickled ginger
- Soy sauce
- Wasabi
- Nori sheets (seaweed)
- Sushi rolls (vegetarian)

Instructions:

1. Arrange bowls of edamame beans, sushi rice, and pickled ginger on a board.
2. Place avocado slices in a small bowl or ramekin.
3. Serve with soy sauce and wasabi in small dishes.
4. Add nori sheets and vegetarian sushi rolls to complete the board.

Middle Eastern Board

- **Prep Time:** 25 minutes
- **Serving Size:** 4-6 people

Ingredients:

- Tabouleh salad
- Baba ganoush
- Falafel balls

- Stuffed grape leaves (dolmas)
- Hummus
- Pita bread or naan bread
- Olives and pickles

Instructions:

1. Arrange bowls of tabouleh salad, baba ganoush, falafel balls, and stuffed grape leaves on a board.
2. Place a bowl of hummus in the center of the board.
3. Serve with pita bread or naan bread.
4. Scatter olives and pickles around the board.

Springtime Freshness Board

- **Prep Time:** 20 minutes
- **Serving Size:** 4-6 people

Ingredients:

- Fresh strawberries and grapes
- Baby carrots and cucumber slices
- Radishes and cherry tomatoes
- Herbed goat cheese
- Balsamic glaze
- Crackers or breadsticks

Instructions:

1. Arrange fresh strawberries, grapes, baby carrots, cucumber slices, radishes, and cherry tomatoes on a board.
2. Place a bowl of herbed goat cheese in the center of the board.
3. Drizzle balsamic glaze over the cheese and vegetables.

4. Serve with crackers or breadsticks.

Breakfast Brunch Board

- **Prep Time:** 25 minutes
- **Serving Size:** 4-6 people

Ingredients:

- Hard-boiled eggs (halved)
- Fresh fruit (berries, melon)
- Yogurt with honey or fruit compote
- Granola
- Mini muffins or scones
- Mixed nuts (almonds, walnuts)

Instructions:

1. Arrange halved hard-boiled eggs, fresh fruit, and small bowls of yogurt with honey or fruit compote on a board.
2. Scatter granola and mixed nuts around the board.
3. Serve with mini muffins or scones.

Chapter 6: Vegan Charcuterie Board Recipes

Classic Vegan Cheese Board

- **Prep Time:** 15 minutes

- **Serving Size:** 4-6 people

Ingredients:

- Assorted vegan cheeses (cashew cheese, almond cheese)

- Grapes

- Cherry tomatoes

- Mixed olives

- Crackers or crusty bread

Instructions:

1. Arrange assorted vegan cheeses on a board.

2. Scatter grapes, cherry tomatoes, and mixed olives around the cheeses.

3. Serve with crackers or crusty bread.

Mediterranean Vegan Mezze Board

- **Prep Time:** 20 minutes

- **Serving Size:** 4-6 people

Ingredients:

- Hummus

- Baba ganoush

- Falafel balls

- Stuffed grape leaves (dolmas)

- Cherry tomatoes

- Cucumber slices

- Pita bread or crackers

Instructions:

1. Arrange bowls of hummus and baba ganoush on a large serving board or platter.

2. Place falafel balls and stuffed grape leaves (dolmas) around the bowls.

3. Scatter cherry tomatoes and cucumber slices over the board.

4. Serve with pita bread or crackers.

Vegan Antipasti Board

- **Prep Time:** 15 minutes
- **Serving Size:** 4-6 people

Ingredients:

- Marinated artichoke hearts
- Roasted red peppers
- Mixed olives
- Cherry tomatoes
- Pickled vegetables (cucumbers, carrots)
- Sliced baguette or breadsticks

Instructions:

1. Arrange marinated artichoke hearts, roasted red peppers, mixed olives, cherry tomatoes, and pickled vegetables on a board.

2. Serve with sliced baguette or breadsticks.

Asian-Inspired Vegan Board

- **Prep Time:** 20 minutes
- **Serving Size:** 4-6 people

Ingredients:

- Edamame beans (steamed and salted)
- Sushi rice
- Avocado slices
- Pickled ginger
- Soy sauce
- Wasabi
- Nori sheets (seaweed)
- Veggie sushi rolls (avocado, cucumber, carrot)

Instructions:

1. Arrange bowls of edamame beans, sushi rice, and pickled ginger on a board.
2. Place avocado slices in a small bowl or ramekin.
3. Serve with soy sauce and wasabi in small dishes.
4. Add nori sheets and veggie sushi rolls to complete the board.

Vegan Cheese Lover's Board

- **Prep Time:** 15 minutes
- **Serving Size:** 4-6 people

Ingredients:

- Assorted vegan cheeses (cashew cheese, almond cheese)
- Fresh fruit (grapes, apples)
- Nuts (walnuts, almonds)

- Dried fruit (apricots, figs)
- Crackers or crusty bread

Instructions:

1. Arrange assorted vegan cheeses on a board.

2. Scatter fresh fruit, nuts, and dried fruit around the cheeses.

3. Serve with crackers or crusty bread.

Mexican-Inspired Vegan Board

- **Prep Time:** 20 minutes
- **Serving Size:** 4-6 people

Ingredients:

- Guacamole
- Salsa
- Refried beans
- Pickled jalapeños
- Fresh cilantro
- Tortilla chips

Instructions:

1. Arrange bowls of guacamole, salsa, and refried beans on a board.

2. Scatter pickled jalapeños and fresh cilantro around the bowls.

3. Serve with tortilla chips for dipping.

Vegan Charcuterie Platter

- **Prep Time:** 15 minutes
- **Serving Size:** 4-6 people

Ingredients:

- Vegan deli slices (such as smoked tofu or seitan)
- Vegan cheese slices or spreads
- Mustard and vegan mayo
- Pickles and olives
- Cherry tomatoes
- Bread or crackers

Instructions:

1. Arrange vegan deli slices and cheese slices or spreads on a platter.
2. Place small bowls of mustard and vegan mayo on the platter.
3. Scatter pickles, olives, and cherry tomatoes around the slices.
4. Serve with bread or crackers.

Vegan Brunch Board

- **Prep Time:** 20 minutes
- **Serving Size:** 4-6 people

Ingredients:

- Hummus
- Avocado slices
- Cherry tomatoes
- Fresh fruit (berries, melon)
- Nuts (almonds, cashews)

- Mini bagels or toast slices

Instructions:

1. Arrange bowls of hummus and avocado slices on a board.

2. Scatter cherry tomatoes, fresh fruit, and nuts around the bowls.

3. Serve with mini bagels or toast slices.

Vegan Dessert Board

- **Prep Time:** 20 minutes

- **Serving Size:** 4-6 people

Ingredients:

- Vegan chocolate truffles

- Fresh strawberries

- Mixed nuts (such as almonds and walnuts)

- Dried fruit (apricots, figs)

- Vegan cookies or biscotti

Instructions:

1. Arrange vegan chocolate truffles, fresh strawberries, mixed nuts, and dried fruit on a board.

2. Serve with vegan cookies or biscotti.

Vegan Holiday Board

- **Prep Time:** 25 minutes
- **Serving Size:** 4-6 people

Ingredients:

- Vegan cheese balls (cashew or almond-based)
- Cranberry sauce
- Mixed nuts (such as pecans and almonds)
- Fresh grapes
- Crackers or breadsticks

Instructions:

1. Arrange vegan cheese balls on a board.
2. Place a bowl of cranberry sauce in the center of the board.
3. Scatter mixed nuts and fresh grapes around the cheese balls.
4. Serve with crackers or breadsticks.

Chapter 7: Drinks and Mix Charcuterie Board Recipes

Mimosa Bar Board

- **Prep Time:** 15 minutes

- **Serving Size:** 4-6 people

Ingredients:

- Champagne or sparkling wine

- Orange juice

- Peach nectar or mango juice

- Fresh berries (strawberries, raspberries)

- Orange slices

Instructions:

1. Arrange bottles of champagne or sparkling wine on a board.

2. Place pitchers or carafes of orange juice and peach nectar or mango juice nearby.

3. Scatter fresh berries and orange slices on the board.

4. Provide glasses and let guests create their own mimosas.

Sangria Board

- **Prep Time:** 20 minutes

- **Serving Size:** 4-6 people

Ingredients:

- Red wine

- White wine

- Orange liqueur (such as Cointreau)

- Fresh citrus fruits (oranges, lemons, limes)

- Fresh berries (strawberries, blueberries)
- Mint leaves

Instructions:

1. Arrange bottles of red wine and white wine on a board.

2. Place a bottle of orange liqueur (e.g., Cointreau) on the board.

3. Scatter slices of fresh citrus fruits, such as oranges, lemons, and limes.

4. Add fresh berries and mint leaves for garnish.

5. Provide glasses and a pitcher for guests to mix their own sangria.

Bloody Mary Bar Board

- **Prep Time:** 20 minutes
- **Serving Size:** 4-6 people

Ingredients:

- Vodka
- Bloody Mary mix
- Tomato juice
- Worcestershire sauce
- Hot sauce
- Celery salt
- Lemon and lime wedges
- Pickles, olives, and celery sticks

Instructions:

1. Arrange bottles of vodka and pitchers of Bloody Mary mix and tomato juice on a board.

2. Place small bowls of Worcestershire sauce, hot sauce, and celery salt nearby.

3. Scatter lemon and lime wedges, along with pickles, olives, and celery sticks.

4. Provide glasses and let guests customize their Bloody Marys.

Mojito Board

- **Prep Time:** 15 minutes
- **Serving Size:** 4-6 people

Ingredients:

- White rum
- Fresh mint leaves
- Limes (cut into wedges)
- Simple syrup or sugar
- Club soda
- Fresh berries (optional garnish)

Instructions:

1. Arrange bottles of white rum and a pitcher of simple syrup or sugar syrup on a board.

2. Place fresh mint leaves and lime wedges on the board.

3. Provide glasses filled with ice cubes.

4. Guests can muddle mint leaves and lime wedges, add rum and simple syrup, then top with club soda to create their mojitos.

5. Optionally, scatter fresh berries for garnish.

Martini Bar Board

- **Prep Time:** 15 minutes
- **Serving Size:** 4-6 people

Ingredients:

- Gin or vodka
- Dry vermouth
- Sweet vermouth (optional)
- Olives (for garnish)
- Lemon twists (for garnish)
- Cocktail picks

Instructions:

1. Arrange bottles of gin or vodka and dry vermouth on a board.
2. Optionally, include a bottle of sweet vermouth.
3. Scatter olives and lemon twists on the board.
4. Provide cocktail picks and glasses chilled with ice.
5. Guests can mix their preferred ratio of gin/vodka and vermouth, garnish with olives or lemon twists.

Coffee and Tea Board

- **Prep Time:** 10 minutes
- **Serving Size:** 4-6 people

Ingredients:

- Assorted teas (black, green, herbal)
- Coffee (brewed and cold brew)
- Milk or dairy-free alternatives (almond milk, oat milk)

- Sweeteners (sugar, honey)

- Lemon slices (for tea)

- Cinnamon sticks (for coffee)

Instructions:

1. Arrange a selection of assorted teas and coffee options (brewed and cold brew) on a board.

2. Provide milk or dairy-free alternatives and sweeteners in small pitchers or bowls.

3. Scatter lemon slices and cinnamon sticks on the board.

4. Guests can brew their preferred tea or coffee, add milk and sweeteners as desired.

Hot Chocolate Bar Board

- **Prep Time:** 15 minutes

- **Serving Size:** 4-6 people

Ingredients:

- Hot chocolate mix or cocoa powder

- Hot water or milk (dairy or dairy-free)

- Whipped cream (vegan if desired)

- Mini marshmallows

- Chocolate shavings or cocoa powder (for garnish)

Instructions:

1. Arrange hot chocolate mix or cocoa powder on a board.

2. Provide hot water or milk (dairy or dairy-free) in a pitcher or carafe.

3. Place bowls of whipped cream (vegan if desired) and mini marshmallows nearby.

4. Scatter chocolate shavings or cocoa powder for garnish.

5. Guests can mix hot chocolate to their desired strength and top with whipped cream, marshmallows, and chocolate shavings.

Smoothie Bar Board

- **Prep Time:** 15 minutes

- **Serving Size:** 4-6 people

Ingredients:

- Assorted frozen fruits (berries, mango, pineapple)

- Fresh spinach or kale (optional)

- Dairy or dairy-free milk (almond milk, coconut milk)

- Protein powder (optional)

- Chia seeds or flaxseeds (optional)

- Honey or agave syrup (optional)

Instructions:

1. Arrange bowls of assorted frozen fruits and fresh greens (if using) on a board.

2. Provide dairy or dairy-free milk in a pitcher or carafe.

3. Include optional ingredients like protein powder, chia seeds, flaxseeds, honey, or agave syrup in small bowls.

4. Guests can blend their preferred combination of fruits, greens, milk, and optional ingredients to create smoothies.

Iced Tea and Lemonade Board

- **Prep Time:** 10 minutes
- **Serving Size:** 4-6 people

Ingredients:

- Iced tea (black, green, or herbal)
- Freshly squeezed lemonade
- Fresh lemon slices
- Fresh mint leaves
- Simple syrup or sugar (optional)

Instructions:

1. Arrange pitchers of iced tea and freshly squeezed lemonade on a board.
2. Scatter fresh lemon slices and mint leaves for garnish.
3. Provide simple syrup or sugar for guests to sweeten their drinks if desired.
4. Guests can mix their preferred ratio of iced tea and lemonade, garnish with lemon slices and mint leaves.

Mocktail Bar Board

- **Prep Time:** 15 minutes
- **Serving Size:** 4-6 people

Ingredients:

- Assorted fruit juices (orange, pineapple, cranberry)
- Club soda or sparkling water
- Fresh fruit slices (lemon, lime, berries)
- Fresh herbs (mint, basil)
- Ice cubes

Instructions:

1. Arrange assorted fruit juices and club soda or sparkling water on a board.

2. Scatter fresh fruit slices and herbs for garnish.

3. Provide glasses filled with ice cubes.

4. Guests can mix their preferred combination of fruit juices and sparkling water, garnish with fresh fruit slices and herbs.

Chapter 8: Sweet Breads

Banana Bread

- **Prep Time:** 15 minutes
- **Cook Time:** 1 hour
- **Serving Size:** 8-10 slices

Ingredients:

- 2-3 ripe bananas, mashed
- 1/3 cup melted butter or vegetable oil
- 1 teaspoon vanilla extract
- 1/2 cup granulated sugar
- 1 egg, beaten
- 1 teaspoon baking soda
- Pinch of salt
- 1 1/2 cups all-purpose flour

Instructions:

1. Preheat your oven to 350°F (175°C). Grease a loaf pan.

2. In a mixing bowl, combine mashed bananas, melted butter or oil, vanilla extract, and sugar.

3. Mix in the beaten egg.

4. Add baking soda and salt, then gradually stir in flour until just incorporated.

5. Pour batter into the prepared loaf pan and bake for 60 minutes, or until a toothpick inserted into the center comes out clean.

6. Let cool in the pan for 10 minutes, then transfer to a wire rack to cool completely before slicing.

Lemon Poppy Seed Bread

- **Prep Time:** 15 minutes
- **Cook Time:** 50 minutes
- **Serving Size:** 8-10 slices

Ingredients:

- 1/2 cup unsalted butter, softened
- 1 cup granulated sugar
- 2 eggs
- 1/2 cup plain yogurt or sour cream
- 1/4 cup fresh lemon juice
- Zest of 1 lemon
- 1 1/2 cups all-purpose flour
- 1 tablespoon poppy seeds
- 1 teaspoon baking powder
- 1/2 teaspoon baking soda
- 1/4 teaspoon salt

Instructions:

1. Preheat your oven to 350°F (175°C). Grease a loaf pan.
2. In a large bowl, cream together butter and sugar until light and fluffy.
3. Beat in eggs, one at a time, then stir in yogurt (or sour cream), lemon juice, and lemon zest.
4. In a separate bowl, whisk together flour, poppy seeds, baking powder, baking soda, and salt.
5. Gradually add dry ingredients to the wet ingredients, mixing until just combined.

6. Pour batter into the prepared loaf pan and bake for 50 minutes, or until a toothpick inserted into the center comes out clean.

7. Cool in the pan for 10 minutes, then transfer to a wire rack to cool completely.

Pumpkin Bread

- **Prep Time:** 15 minutes
- **Cook Time:** 1 hour
- **Serving Size:** 8-10 slices

Ingredients:

- 1 3/4 cups all-purpose flour
- 1 teaspoon baking soda
- 1/2 teaspoon baking powder
- 1/2 teaspoon salt
- 1 teaspoon ground cinnamon
- 1/2 teaspoon ground nutmeg
- 1/2 teaspoon ground cloves
- 1/4 teaspoon ground ginger
- 1/2 cup unsalted butter, melted
- 1 cup granulated sugar
- 1 cup canned pumpkin puree
- 2 eggs, beaten
- 1/4 cup water

Instructions:

1. Preheat your oven to 350°F (175°C). Grease a loaf pan.

2. In a large bowl, whisk together flour, baking soda, baking powder, salt, cinnamon, nutmeg, cloves, and ginger.

3. In another bowl, mix together melted butter, sugar, pumpkin puree, beaten eggs, and water.

4. Stir wet ingredients into the dry ingredients until just combined.

5. Pour batter into the prepared loaf pan and bake for 60 minutes, or until a toothpick inserted into the center comes out clean.

6. Cool in the pan for 10 minutes, then transfer to a wire rack to cool completely.

Zucchini Bread

- **Prep Time:** 15 minutes

- **Cook Time:** 1 hour

- **Serving Size:** 8-10 slices

Ingredients:

- 1 1/2 cups grated zucchini

- 1 cup granulated sugar

- 1/2 cup vegetable oil or melted butter

- 2 eggs

- 1 teaspoon vanilla extract

- 1 1/2 cups all-purpose flour

- 1/2 teaspoon baking powder

- 1/2 teaspoon baking soda

- 1/2 teaspoon salt

- 1 teaspoon ground cinnamon

- 1/2 cup chopped walnuts or pecans (optional)

Instructions:

1. Preheat your oven to 350°F (175°C). Grease a loaf pan.

2. In a large bowl, mix together grated zucchini, sugar, vegetable oil or melted butter, eggs, and vanilla extract.

3. In another bowl, whisk together flour, baking powder, baking soda, salt, and cinnamon.

4. Gradually add dry ingredients to the zucchini mixture, stirring until just combined.

5. Fold in chopped nuts, if using.

6. Pour batter into the prepared loaf pan and bake for 60 minutes, or until a toothpick inserted into the center comes out clean.

7. Cool in the pan for 10 minutes, then transfer to a wire rack to cool completely.

Apple Cinnamon Bread

-   **Prep Time:** 20 minutes

-   **Cook Time:** 1 hour

-   **Serving Size:** 8-10 slices

Ingredients:

-   2 cups all-purpose flour

-   1 teaspoon baking powder

-   1/2 teaspoon baking soda

-   1/2 teaspoon salt

-   1 teaspoon ground cinnamon

-   1/2 cup unsalted butter, softened

-   1 cup granulated sugar

-   2 eggs

- 1 teaspoon vanilla extract

- 1/2 cup milk (dairy or non-dairy)

- 1 1/2 cups peeled and diced apples (such as Granny Smith)

Instructions:

1. Preheat your oven to 350°F (175°C). Grease a loaf pan.

2. In a bowl, whisk together flour, baking powder, baking soda, salt, and ground cinnamon.

3. In a large bowl, cream together softened butter and sugar until light and fluffy.

4. Beat in eggs, one at a time, then stir in vanilla extract.

5. Gradually add dry ingredients to the butter mixture, alternating with milk, until just combined.

6. Fold in diced apples.

7. Pour batter into the prepared loaf pan and bake for 60 minutes, or until a toothpick inserted into the center comes out clean.

8. Cool in the pan for 10 minutes, then transfer to a wire rack to cool completely.

Chocolate Chip Banana Bread

- **Prep Time:** 15 minutes

- **Cook Time:** 1 hour

- **Serving Size:** 8-10 slices

Ingredients:

- 2-3 ripe bananas, mashed

- 1/3 cup melted butter or vegetable oil

- 1 teaspoon vanilla extract

- 1/2 cup granulated sugar

- 1 egg, beaten
- 1 teaspoon baking soda
- Pinch of salt
- 1 1/2 cups all-purpose flour
- 1 cup chocolate chips

Instructions:

1. Preheat your oven to 350°F (175°C). Grease a loaf pan.

2. In a mixing bowl, combine mashed bananas, melted butter or oil, vanilla extract, and sugar.

3. Mix in the beaten egg.

4. Add baking soda and salt, then gradually stir in flour until just incorporated.

5. Fold in chocolate chips.

6. Pour batter into the prepared loaf pan and bake for 60 minutes, or until a toothpick inserted into the center comes out clean.

7. Let cool in the pan for 10 minutes, then transfer to a wire rack to cool completely before slicing.

Orange Cranberry Bread

- **Prep Time:** 15 minutes
- **Cook Time:** 1 hour
- **Serving Size:** 8-10 slices

Ingredients:

- 2 cups all-purpose flour
- 1 teaspoon baking powder
- 1/2 teaspoon baking soda
- 1/2 teaspoon salt

- Zest of 1 orange

- 1/2 cup unsalted butter, softened

- 1 cup granulated sugar

- 2 eggs

- 3/4 cup fresh orange juice

- 1 cup dried cranberries

Instructions:

1. Preheat your oven to 350°F (175°C). Grease a loaf pan.

2. In a bowl, whisk together flour, baking powder, baking soda, salt, and orange zest.

3. In a large bowl, cream together softened butter and sugar until light and fluffy.

4. Beat in eggs, one at a time, then stir in fresh orange juice.

5. Gradually add dry ingredients to the butter mixture, stirring until just combined.

6. Fold in dried cranberries.

7. Pour batter into the prepared loaf pan and bake for 60 minutes, or until a toothpick inserted into the center comes out clean.

8. Cool in the pan for 10 minutes, then transfer to a wire rack to cool completely.

Cinnamon Swirl Bread

- **Prep Time:** 20 minutes

- **Cook Time:** 45 minutes

- **Serving Size:** 8-10 slices

Ingredients:

- 2 cups all-purpose flour

- 1 tablespoon baking powder

- 1/2 teaspoon salt

- 1/2 cup granulated sugar

- 1 cup milk (dairy or non-dairy)

- 1/4 cup vegetable oil or melted butter

- 2 eggs

- 1 teaspoon vanilla extract

- 1/2 cup packed brown sugar

- 1 1/2 teaspoons ground cinnamon

Instructions:

1. Preheat your oven to 350°F (175°C). Grease a loaf pan.

2. In a bowl, whisk together flour, baking powder, and salt.

3. In another bowl, whisk together granulated sugar, milk, vegetable oil or melted butter, eggs, and vanilla extract.

4. Gradually add dry ingredients to the wet ingredients, mixing until just combined.

5. In a small bowl, mix brown sugar and ground cinnamon.

6. Pour half of the batter into the prepared loaf pan. Sprinkle half of the cinnamon sugar mixture over the batter.

7. Pour the remaining batter over the cinnamon sugar layer. Sprinkle the remaining cinnamon sugar mixture on top.

8. Use a knife to swirl the cinnamon sugar mixture into the batter.

9. Bake for 45 minutes, or until a toothpick inserted into the center comes out clean.

10. Cool in the pan for 10 minutes, then transfer to a wire rack to cool completely.

Almond Poppy Seed Bread

- **Prep Time:** 15 minutes
- **Cook Time:** 1 hour
- **Serving Size:** 8-10 slices

Ingredients:

- 1/2 cup unsalted butter, softened
- 1 cup granulated sugar
- 2 eggs
- 1 teaspoon almond extract
- 1 1/2 cups all-purpose flour
- 1 teaspoon baking powder
- 1/2 teaspoon baking soda
- 1/4 teaspoon salt
- 1/2 cup milk (dairy or non-dairy)
- 2 tablespoons poppy seeds

Instructions:

1. Preheat your oven to 350°F (175°C). Grease a loaf pan.

2. In a large bowl, cream together softened butter and sugar until light and fluffy.

3. Beat in eggs, one at a time, then stir in almond extract.

4. In another bowl, whisk together flour, baking powder, baking soda, and salt.

5. Gradually add dry ingredients to the butter mixture, alternating with milk, until just combined.

6. Stir in poppy seeds.

7. Pour batter into the prepared loaf pan and bake for 60 minutes, or until a toothpick inserted into the center comes out clean.

8. Cool in the pan for 10 minutes, then transfer to a wire rack to cool completely.

Coconut Bread

- **Prep Time:** 15 minutes
- **Cook Time:** 1 hour
- **Serving Size:** 8-10 slices

Ingredients:

- 1/2 cup unsalted butter, softened
- 1 cup granulated sugar
- 2 eggs
- 1 teaspoon vanilla extract
- 1 1/2 cups all-purpose flour
- 1 teaspoon baking powder
- 1/4 teaspoon baking soda
- 1/4 teaspoon salt
- 1/2 cup milk (dairy or non-dairy)

- 1 cup shredded sweetened coconut

Instructions:

1. Preheat your oven to 350°F (175°C). Grease a loaf pan.

2. In a large bowl, cream together softened butter and sugar until light and fluffy.

3. Beat in eggs, one at a time, then stir in vanilla extract.

4. In another bowl, whisk together flour, baking powder, baking soda, and salt.

5. Gradually add dry ingredients to the butter mixture, alternating with milk, until just combined.

6. Stir in shredded coconut.

7. Pour batter into the prepared loaf pan and bake for 60 minutes, or until a toothpick inserted into the center comes out clean.

8. Cool in the pan for 10 minutes, then transfer to a wire rack to cool completely.

Chapter 9: Sauces, Condiments & Dips for Charcuterie Boards

Classic Hummus

- **Prep Time:** 10 minutes
- **Serving Size:** Makes about 1 1/2 cups

Ingredients:

- 1 can (15 ounces) chickpeas, drained and rinsed
- 1/4 cup tahini
- 1/4 cup fresh lemon juice
- 1 clove garlic, minced
- 2 tablespoons olive oil
- 1/2 teaspoon ground cumin
- Salt and pepper, to taste
- Water (as needed for consistency)

Instructions:

1. In a food processor, combine chickpeas, tahini, lemon juice, garlic, olive oil, and cumin.
2. Process until smooth, adding water gradually to achieve desired consistency.
3. Season with salt and pepper to taste.
4. Transfer hummus to a serving bowl and drizzle with olive oil before serving.

Garlic Aioli

- **Prep Time:** 5 minutes
- **Serving Size:** Makes about 1 cup

Ingredients:

- 1 cup mayonnaise
- 2 cloves garlic, minced
- 1 tablespoon lemon juice
- Salt and pepper, to taste

Instructions:

1. In a bowl, whisk together mayonnaise, minced garlic, and lemon juice until well combined.
2. Season with salt and pepper to taste.
3. Cover and refrigerate for at least 30 minutes to allow flavors to meld before serving.

Spicy Mango Chutney

- **Prep Time:** 10 minutes
- **Cook Time:** 20 minutes
- **Serving Size:** Makes about 1 cup

Ingredients:

- 1 ripe mango, peeled and diced
- 1/4 cup white vinegar
- 1/4 cup brown sugar
- 1/4 cup raisins
- 1/2 teaspoon ground ginger
- 1/4 teaspoon ground cinnamon

- Pinch of cayenne pepper (adjust to taste)

- Salt, to taste

Instructions:

1. In a saucepan, combine diced mango, white vinegar, brown sugar, raisins, ground ginger, ground cinnamon, and cayenne pepper.

2. Bring mixture to a boil over medium-high heat, stirring occasionally.

3. Reduce heat to low and simmer for about 15-20 minutes, or until chutney thickens.

4. Season with salt to taste.

5. Let cool completely before serving.

Herbed Yogurt Dip

- **Prep Time:** 5 minutes
- **Serving Size:** Makes about 1 cup

Ingredients:

- 1 cup Greek yogurt

- 1 tablespoon chopped fresh dill

- 1 tablespoon chopped fresh parsley

- 1 tablespoon chopped fresh chives

- 1 tablespoon lemon juice

- Salt and pepper, to taste

Instructions:

1. In a bowl, combine Greek yogurt, chopped dill, parsley, chives, and lemon juice.

2. Stir until herbs are evenly distributed.

3. Season with salt and pepper to taste.

4. Refrigerate for at least 30 minutes to allow flavors to meld before serving.

Balsamic Fig Jam

- **Prep Time:** 5 minutes

- **Cook Time:** 20 minutes

- **Serving Size:** Makes about 1 cup

Ingredients:

- 1 cup dried figs, stemmed and chopped

- 1/2 cup water

- 1/4 cup balsamic vinegar

- 2 tablespoons honey

- Pinch of salt

Instructions:

1. In a saucepan, combine chopped dried figs, water, balsamic vinegar, honey, and a pinch of salt.

2. Bring mixture to a boil over medium-high heat.

3. Reduce heat to low and simmer, stirring occasionally, for about 15-20 minutes, or until figs are softened and jam thickens.

4. Remove from heat and let cool before serving.

Sun-Dried Tomato Pesto

- **Prep Time:** 10 minutes

- **Serving Size:** Makes about 1 cup

Ingredients:

- 1 cup sun-dried tomatoes (packed in oil), drained

- 1/2 cup grated Parmesan cheese

- 1/4 cup pine nuts or walnuts

- 2 cloves garlic

- 1/4 cup olive oil

- Salt and pepper, to taste

Instructions:

1. In a food processor, combine sun-dried tomatoes, Parmesan cheese, pine nuts or walnuts, and garlic.

2. Pulse until ingredients are finely chopped.

3. With the processor running, slowly drizzle in olive oil until pesto reaches desired consistency.

4. Season with salt and pepper to taste.

5. Transfer to a serving bowl and drizzle with additional olive oil before serving.

Caramelized Onion Dip

- **Prep Time:** 10 minutes

- **Cook Time:** 30 minutes

- **Serving Size:** Makes about 1 1/2 cups

Ingredients:

- 2 large onions, thinly sliced

- 2 tablespoons olive oil

- 1 cup sour cream

- 1/2 cup mayonnaise

- 1 teaspoon Worcestershire sauce

- Salt and pepper, to taste

Instructions:

1. In a large skillet, heat olive oil over medium heat.

2. Add thinly sliced onions and cook, stirring occasionally, until onions are caramelized and golden brown, about 25-30 minutes.

3. Remove from heat and let cool.

4. In a bowl, combine caramelized onions, sour cream, mayonnaise, and Worcestershire sauce.

5. Season with salt and pepper to taste.

6. Refrigerate for at least 1 hour before serving to allow flavors to meld.

Roasted Red Pepper Dip

- **Prep Time:** 10 minutes

- **Cook Time:** 20 minutes (if roasting peppers)

- **Serving Size:** Makes about 1 1/2 cups

Ingredients:

- 2 large red bell peppers

- 1 cup Greek yogurt

- 1/4 cup mayonnaise

- 1 clove garlic, minced

- 1 tablespoon lemon juice

- Salt and pepper, to taste

Instructions:

1. If roasting peppers: Preheat broiler. Place red bell peppers on a baking sheet and broil, turning occasionally, until skins are charred and blistered. Remove from oven, place in a bowl, cover with plastic wrap, and let steam for 10 minutes. Peel off charred skins, remove seeds and stems, then chop peppers.

2. In a food processor, combine chopped roasted red peppers, Greek yogurt, mayonnaise, minced garlic, and lemon juice.

3. Pulse until smooth.

4. Season with salt and pepper to taste.

5. Transfer to a serving bowl and refrigerate until ready to serve.

Avocado Lime Crema

- **Prep Time:** 5 minutes

- **Serving Size:** Makes about 1 cup

Ingredients:

- 1 ripe avocado, peeled and pitted

- 1/2 cup sour cream or Greek yogurt

- Juice of 1 lime

- 1 clove garlic, minced

- Salt and pepper, to taste

Instructions:

1. In a bowl, mash ripe avocado until smooth.

2. Stir in sour cream or Greek yogurt, lime juice, and minced garlic until well combined.

3. Season with salt and pepper to taste.

4. Refrigerate for at least 30 minutes before serving to allow flavors to meld.

Buffalo Blue Cheese Dip

- **Prep Time:** 5 minutes

- **Serving Size:** Makes about 1 cup

Ingredients:

- 1/2 cup mayonnaise

- 1/2 cup sour cream or Greek yogurt

- 1/4 cup buffalo sauce (adjust to taste)

- 1/4 cup crumbled blue cheese

- 1/2 teaspoon garlic powder

- Salt and pepper, to taste

Instructions:

1. In a bowl, whisk together mayonnaise, sour cream or Greek yogurt, buffalo sauce, crumbled blue cheese, garlic powder, salt, and pepper until smooth.

2. Adjust buffalo sauce to taste for desired spiciness.

3. Refrigerate for at least 30 minutes before serving to allow flavors to meld.

Conclusion

Creating the perfect charcuterie board is an art form that requires creativity, diversity, and attention to detail. With the recipes and techniques presented in this booklet, you now have the skills to build delectable and visually spectacular charcuterie boards for any occasion. Whether you're preparing a simple spread for a casual party or an intricate arrangement for a major event, the possibilities are unlimited.

The key to a perfect charcuterie board is in balancing flavors, textures, and colors. From the rich, savory meats and creamy cheeses to the fresh, vivid fruits and crunchy nuts, every element plays a critical role in creating a balanced and appealing presentation. Don't forget the value of sauces, condiments, and dips, which may heighten the experience by adding depth and complexity to each bite.

Remember to personalize your boards to meet the interests of your visitors, presenting a choice of alternatives that appeal to varied tastes and dietary demands. Whether it's a vegetarian, vegan, or typical charcuterie board, the goal is to deliver a memorable and delightful experience for everyone.

As you discover the world of charcuterie, don't be hesitant to experiment with new ingredients, pairings, and configurations. Use the core information and recipes in this cookbook as a starting point, but allow your creativity and personal touch come through. The delight of charcuterie is in the countless permutations and the possibility to share exquisite moments with friends and family.

Thank you for choosing this booklet as your guide to quick charcuterie boards. We hope it encourages you to make attractive, savory spreads that bring people together and celebrate the art of grazing. Enjoy every tasty bite, and happy charcuterie creation!